Silence No More

Kenisha Burke

ISBN:9781365009099
ISBN-13:978-1365-00909-0

DEDICATION

This book is dedicated to love because love is the first step. Once you learn to love yourself everything else follows.

CONTENTS

ACKNOWLEDGMENTS

To love of my life, thanks for helping me find the courage to tell my truth!

MY TRUTH

I have sat down to write this story many times and most of them have been failed attempts. To write the story of what is really a very short life packed with so many tragic and beautiful experiences is a difficult task. This is my recollection of several events that occurred in my life, it might not be what all parties involved feel happened. This is however my story, the one I consider part of my life and I decided that I am going to tell it my way and on my terms. This story does not include my entire life or every event that occurred but it is me sharing the memories that made me the woman I am today. You will see that I don't engage in dialogue but I write this story in my voice from my perspective. What silence does to you is it prevents you from having a perspective on your life because you are forced not to say what is happening in your now. So for many this may not be the way you feel this story should be told but I don't care. I was silenced as a child and told not to share our business with world. Most of the time I walked away from writing this story out of fear, fear of losing my family and never being able to talk to them again. I thought that my silence would keep the people I loved close and they would at least love me for it. The funny thing is that without me telling my truth or this story out loud it allowed those people to mistreat me. They were allowed to live as if my pain was not real and I suffered because of that. Being silent caused me nothing but pain and the family I wanted to love me they decided that my presence was a stain on what would be a perfect family, so they excluded me anyway. My abuser has been allowed to celebrate and live in moments that I only dreamed I could be a part of. One of the many issues survivors of child hood sexual abuse face is dealing with family after the truth has been told. Many of us spend our lives in isolation and with no one to turn to. The silence holds us hostage and allows us to stay in the role of victim.

Especially when your family refuses to remove the person from their lives that committed the abuse. So this is me taking my power back, it does not matter if one book is sold, what does matter is I have told my story. I am speaking for so many who have sat across the table from a favorite uncle, cousin or family friend wondering how it was possible no one could see the monster lurking within. I am writing this story for all the women I met along the way that have been afraid to tell their truth. For those women and girls who have been made to sit in silence while dealing with their abusers on a daily basis. I am also choosing to share experiences in my life that we don't talk about that I think we are silenced about or are considered taboo topics.

I would like to take the time to thank my husband for standing by me through all the trials and tribulations my history has brought into our lives. For holding me at night through nightmares and loving me unconditionally. I would also like to thank my children for allowing me the opportunity to be a mother when I had no idea it would ever be possible. If you don't know it now you will soon learn that dreams don't have to be dream when you are willing to work hard to accomplish your goals.

I also have to thank the women in my life, the mothers I have, who never gave birth to me. The sisters I have that are not related by blood. These women have been a part of my healing. Some of them have been in my life for moments and others for years. The spirit and compassion of each of these women was there for me during the toughest times in my life. I am a firm believer that every person enters your life for a reason. Each of you came into my life at the right time. If you're still reading, then I want you to know this is my truth. Silence will not dominate my life anymore, I am telling my story, I am telling my truth.

THE CAUSE

To be completely honest I don't remember most of my childhood, just bits and pieces. The memories that I do have are really the most traumatic ones. My earliest memory is standing in an apartment with my mother, she was ironing a shirt, I had to be about 3 or 4 years old but I remember this moment so clearly. I was standing in front of the ironing board and my stepfather at the time came after her. They started to fight and then she hit him with the iron. I can never clearly see his face but I remember being so afraid of him at that moment. That memory has stayed with me for most of my life. It is a clear memory, I can see so much detail about the room and the ironing board each and every time I think about. It is like I am right back in that moment.

After that incident my childhood memories take me to, closets and bathrooms where we would hide from him. I remember a bathroom we were in that had a tub filled with dirty dishes and there were roaches crawling up the walls.

One of my mother's friends had a very nasty house and it seemed like whenever we were hiding from her husband it was in that filthy environment. We were not alone; my mother's boyfriend and future husband was hiding with us. I could never understand why another man would hide with us, it seemed strange that he would not stand up to the man my mother was afraid of. I don't remember having much contact with him at that time, I just remember being afraid of him. My mother used to tell me the story of when I met him. I don't have any recollection of meeting him for the first time. But I was told that I stood in front of the room and said "You know God don't like ugly". I was supposedly only three years old at that time. As an adult I feel like that was a warning sign, maybe somehow a message that was that was sent through a child. I guess everyone thought it was funny, that maybe I was just regurgitating information that I had heard from the adults in my life. As many of my elders would say listening to "grown folks" business and repeating it, like I was grown.

I think it is important to point out that before my mother married my stepfather we had a lot of people in our lives. My mother had friends and cousins who we would see on a daily basis. Slowly throughout their marriage we moved farther away from and lost contact with all the people who used to be present in our lives. My mother started acting as if no one was worthy of being in our presence. As an adult I now know that what was happening was the process of isolation. The smaller of a support system that my mother had, the less likely it would be that she would be strong enough to protect me from the abuse. She was the only person in my life that I relied on other than my grandparents because it was just us. The mother I remember was encouraging and loving until things started to change in her life and she married the man who is my abuser. Her nature has always been to be a helper, so she would take in anyone and help people with abandon. I think these qualities are what allowed her to become the spouse of a man whose intention was to hurt others. It actually appeared to outsiders that my mother was the dominating force in their relationship. Miraculously out of no where she decided that she no longer wanted friends or family. The one thing that was apparent through out my life was that she was angry and suffering in silence. When you become an adult and look back on your life begin to see the answers to question you had that never had an answer before. From the time I could talk, that is all I did was talk. It was my gift and along with it came an imagination. I would sit for hours and read stories and get lost in them. Then I would turn around and write my own story about characters that seemed to live in my head. I was so excited about my ideas and I knew that was my gift. As a very talkative child, I felt like I was not a very well liked or appreciated child. Most of my life I have been told I talked too much, or as the kids would say to me that I ran my mouth 24/7. One of my great uncles would tell me every time that he saw me that I talked too much. He would also tell me that I thought too much of myself and I need to find a corner to sit in and be quiet. I had no idea why he felt that way about me but I do remember thinking that I hated him. As an adult I never made contact with him and pretty much stayed away from him. Every time

I heard that I talked too much my spirit was broken I spent so much of my life trying to make myself smaller and quieter. It was difficult task because I was naturally vibrant, I had a natural ability that would shine through no matter how hard I tried to hide it. Part of my life, was talking too much and it was one of scarlet letters that I wore. I can't say that alone caused major damage in my life but coupled with the sexual abuse I suffered it created a silence that took up most of the space in my life.

My first complete memory of abuse was the summer of 1991; I was getting ready to turn twelve. I say complete because I have bits and pieces of memories that are not clear enough to decipher or share. They are like snippets that flash into my mind then blur away. Many times theses snippets occur in my dreams and they blur together causing horrific nightmares. So I always wanted to be awake more than I wanted to sleep, if given the option. The summer of 1991 we were living in a two family house on the south side of town. I will never forget that house because it had a window seat in the dining room and I use to look out that window and try to look up at the stars. We lived in the upstairs apartment that had access to the attic. My stepfather had set up his music upstairs, a turntable, cassette player and these big Yamaha speakers. He would go up there play music, smoke his cigarettes and drink beer or Southern Comfort. In all actuality it was probably any alcohol that he had at the time. He drank like a fish, that coupled with smoking and bad oral hygiene created a smell that I will never forget, the stench used to ooze through his pores. It became my alarm that he was coming because that smell alerted me to his presence.

Around this time, he would call me upstairs when he was drinking and playing music. Sometime he would be alone but there were many time his brothers or friends would be there too. He would play some old reggae music or new pop and I would dance and listen to music. At least that is how I like to remember it, but in reality it became something of a nightmare. I remember going up in the attic was always scary because the speakers were set up in the doorway so that the entrance was narrowed. He would always stand next to one of the speaker so that as I entered the room he could rub his erection up against me. I remember one day when I walking up the stairs, he was standing in that entrance summoning me to come to him. He would would never move out the way, it did not mater who was there. No one seemed to pay any attention to what he was doing. I was uncomfortable, scary as he rubbed his erect penis up against me when I slid into the attic. I can still remember the fear, the fear of him getting too close to me. If I am honest with myself, I had the fear of him being close to me even before then because it seemed that he would manufacture reasons for me to touch him. It made me so uncomfortable but I was not sure what was wrong, the feeling was so unfamiliar I did not know what to do with it. He was priming me for what he intended to do to me, by seeing what I would do in those moments. I had no idea there was more to come than what was happening. Whenever we were in the same room he would find a reason to brush up against me. His stench hung in the air, as he got closer and I could feel my heart start to pound and my stomach would begin doing flips as he got closer to me every single time even as an adult.

I knew at this time that something was wrong but I did not know how to verbalize it. I was afraid to be alone with him and I would annoy my mother by asking to go wherever she was going. I tried my best not to be in the living room with him, so I would pull my T.V. out as far as it would stretch from my room so I could see the television while I ate dinner. One day while the television was in the door way he walked by and stepped on the cord. The television fell and broke, it was this JVC television that I adored. My mother was pissed at me and said that the next television I got would be one would I purchased myself. I never told her that he broke the television because it seemed like it would not matter anyway. It was impossible for me to go everywhere with my mother and when I was young she worked a lot. This was a part of my daily life so I had no other option but to live with it.

The Friday before my twelfth birthday my stepfather's brother and children came in from out of town, they stopped over and visited with us for a while and then invited us down to us down for the weekend. I am not sure how it happened but it ended up being just my stepfather and I. As I said before, he would manufacture reasons for me to touch him, so for some time he had been asking me to take off his smelly socks and shoes. Promising that he would give me a hundred dollars to spend at the mall. So the premise of this trip was to allow me to spend that money and be rewarded for my good deeds.

I want you to keep in mind I had never been anywhere outside of my hometown before. In fact, I rarely went anywhere other than the houses of family members, local stores and as I got older the homes of the few friends that I had. So I was really excited about the idea of leaving but afraid at the same time. My stepfather had already been drinking and when it was time to get in the car and he made a big deal out of where I sat in the mini van. I wanted to sit as far away from him as possible. So I tried to sit on the complete other side of the car. He made it seem like having one of the boys sit next to him was a problem. In the end I had to switch places with one of his nephews. The first part of the ride down was horrible, he kept trying to touch me as we rode in the dark and I was so afraid. He would paw at my legs or the edge of my shirt and I would shift away from him. I was in a car full of people but it seemed like no one knew I was distressed. I felt like my voice was gone for most of the trip until I mustard up the courage to say that I had to use the bathroom. When we stopped for a bathroom break, he kept looking at me like it was clear that he knew why I said I had to go to the bathroom. I was able to switch places with one of the boys when we got back in the car. I could see in the dark car as we rode, that he knew I did it on purpose because he gave a look that said it all.

After we switched seats I was able to enjoy the ride and the excitement took over, I was going to new place and I was excited. I think it is important to say I was child, I hate when people assume there was some way for me to prevent what happened next, in fact I used to feel like this was my fault However, after becoming a mother and seeing my children go from a scary situation in to jubilation in a split second. I now know how it is possible that children are not thinking about what will happen if they do or don't do something. They live in the moment most of the time.

When we arrived at their house it was late but I was so excited. They boys went upstairs to bed but I wanted to stay downstairs and listen to the adults talk. So I said I would sleep downstairs on the couch. The adults sat and talked for a while but soon decided it was time to turn in.

I remember laying on the floor on my pallet thinking about what tomorrow would bring. Then I felt his hands grabbing at my panties, and soon his penis rubbing up against my skin. I jumped up and screamed and ran into the bathroom and locked the door. I screamed and cried for my mother, saying that I wanted to go home. His sister-in-law was outside the door but so was he; she was asking what was wrong. I kept shouting that I wanted to go home. I could hear him outside the door saying that, I was just homesick because I had never been away from home before I screamed and cried for my mother. Eventually the phone was passed to me in bathroom with with my mother on the other end and she talked me in to staying until morning. I was sent upstairs to lay in one of the boy's room. I was numb and I did not sleep at all that night, I just kept watching the door. I remember seeing the room go from dark to twilight and then seeing the sun come up. Most of that day was a blur but what I remember clearly was him handing me a hundred-dollar bill. I was numb when he gave it to me, like it was payment. His sister-in law took me to the mall with that money. On the car ride with her, I kept trying to decide if I should tell her what really happened. I decide that I would wait until I got home and as soon as we were alone telling my mother. I did not know if I could really trust this woman. Honestly I don't remember even spending the money, I just can feel as I type the numbness that took over my body as I sat in the car with that money in my hand. I avoid handling hundred-dollar bills even now; I will ask that it is broken down or give it away as soon as possible. The rest of the time I spent in Rochester is filled with blankness but the only feeling that I carry from that time is the shattering of my will and ability to see myself as a person worth more than a one-hundred-dollar bill.

When I arrived home as soon as I was alone with my mother I told her what happened. I cannot remember what her face looked like when I told her. I know that she walked out of the after I told her. She returned with a big smile and him in tow, they told me that it was not him. She said that it was someone else was in the room and he did it. He kept trying to explain the location of everyone in the room, saying that there was no way it was him. This fictional man that was in the room had violated me and I could not believe that she was entertaining this. They however did not call the police on the imaginary predator that has violated me that night though. She believed that lie and she was convinced that her husband was innocent. I was numb and confused, I though for sure she would believe me and protect me. Instead she was helping him to make sense of how it was impossible for him to be the perpetrator.

As I sat in the living room, I stopped listening to them and began to wonder if I could call my father. He had never really been in my life. At that point in my life I can only remember seeing him three times. I used to daydream that he would come for me and call me his little princess. I would make up stories and tell my classmates he was millionaire or in the mafia. I mean I would come up with the most unbelievable stories about who this man was but they were all grounded in the theory that eventually he would be my salvation.

So after my mother was convinced that she had proven her husband had not abused me she decided it was time to tell me about my father. That we had something in common, she had been in the same situation I was in before. She looked me in the eyes and told me that my father had raped her. That I was the product of that rape and so she knew how I felt, that she sympathized with my feelings. That moment right there changed my life; I was thinking I could call my father. That he would save me once I told him what was going on but now she was telling me that he was the same as my stepfather. To be honest that conversation that we had, said so many things to me. It let me know that I was alone and that I had no one who could save me.

I had grandparents, who were foster parents. From my perspective the children that lived in the foster care system had a horrible life. I saw the system through a lenses that was distorted by my personal experience. In my mind, the life those children were living was worse than living in my own home. Everyone I knew in the system was unhappy and abused, I knew that if I told anyone else, what would happen eventually is that I would end up foster care or living with one of my relatives. There was not one that I would live with, other than my aunt and she lived with my Grandparents too. In my young mind this solidified the idea that I was alone in this and that I would not have anyone to turn to.

Ironically, the very next day my mother left me alone with him so that she could go to work. It was my birthday and when I was walked out of my room, he was laying naked on the living room with an erection covered only by a thin sheet. He summoned me over and I went to him. I have replayed this one scene in my mind so many times. Thinking that, I somehow contributed to that moment and I felt so much guilt. Later that day my uncle came and picked us up so that we could go pick up my birthday cake. I thought at time that maybe I should tell him but with my stepfather in the car I could not get the words out of my mouth. I walked around the house numb and wondering if I should tell my mother again but then decided against it when she called home that afternoon. My mother heard in my voice that something was wrong and she told me that we would celebrate my birthday when she got home, she also told me to stop worrying. I don't remember much of my birthday that year. It was by far the worst one that I had in my young life and I honestly just wanted to forget it. A couple of days later, I remember my mother standing in the kitchen on the phone, my aunt a cousin was in the kitchen with her. We we received a phone call that my cousin who was just a year older than me had died. We used to play together all the time, she had a twin sister and their birthdays were two days before mine. At one point her mother and my mother were two like peas in the pod. We used to live in the same apartment complex and see each other every single day. It seemed like my world just kept getting smaller. Before my stepfather we were always around a lot of people. We had friends and family around all the time. With him in our life we slowly were moved farther away from from the people in our lives that meant something. The death of my cousin pushed me farther into desolation. I would lay in my room and just cry for hours because I just did not know what to do. The last time I saw her we were driving away and she was yelling I love you. She was the only person who ever told me that she loved me at the time in my life. I have no memory of hearing those words from my mother until I was an adult. I was so upset at myself that I did not know how special those moments were. I felt guilty because I had not seen her in a while. That I had not told her I love you back and that I thought it was strange that she said it all the time. I like to believe that she was an angel that was not meant for this earth, she was too pure. The best thing God did was bring her home and away from this cruel world. As I look back she was suffering in the same way I was. Dealing with abuse and family dysfunction right along with epilepsy. She was the first person that died in my life that I had a relationship with and the pain was unbearable.

Her funeral for me was the beginning of a long period in my life where I felt, I was alone. I remember laying on the upstairs porch at my grandmother house after the funeral and just crying for hours. I was crying because of everything I had learned and the grief was just too heavy to keep inside. When I came down stair my great-uncle informed me that me grief was not that bad and I needed to give it a rest.

After her death and the switch was flipped I began to see myself in a whole different light, I did not want to smile anymore. I remember standing in the bathroom looking at my face and refusing to smile because I thought I was ugly. If you look back at many of my school pictures, you will see that I refused to smile. I would stand in my mirror and stare at my face and wish there was a way to change it. I thought that I was ugly and smiling just made my face look worse. To make matters worse my mother had given me a Jerri curl around the time I was five and she kept it in my hair long after it was fashionable. So when comparing myself to other girls everything about me was wrong. It did not help that I endured follow the drip jokes, from family and kids at school.

The incidents with my stepfather had begun to pile up and I really had no idea what to do with them. We moved from south side to the north side of town before the school year started and I thought things might change. My aunt and cousin had come to live with us. My cousin was staying in my room, so I was relegated to the couch. My aunt was staying in the basement with her children. I was hoping for a new start so I asked to go to school on that side of town, that way I could l reinvent myself. Switching schools was a disaster I tried to have a voice in school, so I would raise my hand and answer questions. That did not fare well will some of my classmates and I was teased and bullied. Eventually I switch back to the school on the other side of town and resumed my role as the ugly fat girl. With my aunt and cousins living with us someone had to give up their room for people to have a place to sleep. It never failed that it was me, that I would have to give up my room. So I would sleep on the couch and ask my mother everyday when I would get my room back. Sleeping on the couch meant that he had easy access to me at night. Sleep seemed like a distant thing and I was afraid to close my eyes at night.

One Saturday while I was playing on the floor with all the kids he decides to join us. I think all the mothers had left to go to the grocery store and so he came into the living room wearing just his boxers. I knew once I saw him coming that he was going to try something. He initiated some play wrestling, which resulted with him pinning me to the ground several times and rubbing himself up against me. This went on for longer than it should have and no one was there to save me. You would think with all the adults in that house that I should have been safe. I decide that I would tell my mother again that day because she had to believe me this time, I had witnesses. He had done a lot of things to me when we were alone. No one else was in the room for him to blame this on and she had to believe me.

Let me just say that I don't remember having that conversation with my mother again but remember the outcome. She was mad at me and I am not even sure if she said something to him about. As I sit here I could rehash every single incident that I remember occurring with my stepfather but I don't think it is necessary, I think what is important to says is that he violated me more times than I care to remember or even say. He even manipulated other people in my life to be a part of this abuse. I am not sure if they were complicit or just stupid but in reality some of them were just children themselves.

By the time I became a teenager, my self- image and goals were based around being successful and going to college. In my mind that was the way to get away from all of the trauma that was happening in my life but in the back of my mind I never thought I would get there. In fact, I knew I would not get there because I wanted to die, to cease to exist and become dust. I used to sit and think of ways to kill myself, hoping that with my death my mother would see how wrong she was. In fact, I would daydream about who would come to my funeral and how many people would actually mourn my death. I was so broken and beat down that simplest thing could make me cry or make me fly off the handle. I you said anything even remotely negative to me I would burst into tears and so not only did I talk too much but I was a crybaby too!

When I turned sixteen I met my first boyfriend while I was having a rare visit at my cousin's house. I thought I was in love, for me he was salvation. We had a childish relationship and I used to pour all my anger and emotions into him. He never seemed to mind and was always very sweet about my emotions. Too me just kissing him was enough because I did not see anything else as an option. He was not pressuring me to do anything else either he was really a nice kid. One day while I was at my grandparent's house he called me, I was surprised because I did not know he even had the number. I was even stranger that he would call my grandparents' house. During that phone call he asked me to have sex with him and I was confused. We had never had a conversation about having sex before and this just seemed to come out of the blue. I thought it was the oddest time for him to be asking me to have sex anyway while I was at my grand parent's house. I explained to him that I did not know how, you would think after all the abuse I would have a clue.

The reality is that I was sheltered and naïve and I did not associate what my stepfather was doing to me with sex. Since my stepfather was never able to actually have intercourse with me, I did not even know how to do it. I was a virgin and I had not even thought about losing my virginity. I was more into kissing and holding hands than I was into to sex at that time. We ended the phone call with a promise to talk about it later. My boyfriend was very close to my stepfather; his own father was not present in his life. So my stepfather would take him fishing with us or sometime he would take him alone. He acted like he was a friend to him instead of my father and I think he fell for it. That evening when I returned home, my boyfriend was there and he told me that my stepfather told him to make that call. I was mortified because I knew he was in my relationship and controlling the one person in my life that I thought loved me. After telling me that he left and my stepfather approached me that night, letting me know that he knew my boyfriend had asked me to have sex. I told him that I was not interested and did not even know how to do it. He told me he could fix that and would make sure I could do it. I was just stunned and afraid up until this moment he had done things that were horrible but not as deep as this. I did not want to have sex because he said I had to do it and I tried to really steer clear of him. We were now living in the valley far away from everyone we knew and it was next to impossible to avoid him. The following Saturday while my mother was out he said he was going to show me something. I was sitting in the basement watching television and he put a tape in the VCR. It was porn and he went step by step with the video on how to have sex, and even explained that I should give my boyfriend oral sex first so it would last longer when we got to intercourse. I was scared shitless at that moment and he was staring at me like he had just won the super bowl. Shortly thereafter my mother came home and he snatched that tape out of the VCR and left the room. He used to hide the tapes in the crawl space above the garage. I went to my room after that and lay on my bed and cried, I knew that this was going to happen weather I wanted it too or not. That evening my boyfriend appeared unannounced and came down in the basement. My stepfather was behind him and said that we have privacy right now don't worry about it. I remember feeling defeated at that moment, I loved my boyfriend but I did not want to have sex. That night with my stepfather peering down the stairs, I performed oral sex on my teenage boyfriend then lost my virginity. Shortly after that incident I broke up with my boyfriend and broke my own heart in the same moment.

To be honestly it seemed like every guy that I dated easily became fast friends with my stepfather. As soon as it seemed they were all buddy buddy, he would manufacture some reason for this young man to ask me to have sex. He would try to make it seem like he was doing us a favor. I would break up with them as soon as the sex talk started. Every boy that came into my life seemed to come with the possibility of having my step father control another part of my life. So I stopped dating people that I though he might be able to control or that I might like for that matter. I would participate in short flings that really only meant having sex which is what I thought in my mind what determined my worth. I did not walk around and have meaningless sex with lots of men. It really was on a few but that was too many and they were too old to be having sex with me anyway. So in a way I was being repeatedly raped every time I had sex with someone.

I did not even enjoy sexual intercourse and I was afraid of oral sex because of my first sexual experience. So when I was having sex it was not really because I wanted to do it. I was doing it because it seemed that was what I was supposed to do. It was not even enjoyable; I was just going through the motions because that meant there was possibility someone might like me. I learned very quickly that the men who were willing to have sex with me quickly were not really interested in me at all. I had my heart broken and quickly decided to give up on sex and men completely.

The absence of a boy to manipulate and do his dirty work, made it so that soon he returned to his old tactics. One night while I was sitting down stairs on the couch watching a movie. This man stood up in front of me pulled out his erect penis and asked me to give him oral sex. He said that he would buy me a car if I did it, he kept moving closer and closer me and it was at that moment that I snapped. He was begging me to suck him off and he had his penis in my face. I jumped over the back of couch and ran upstairs.

I was numb and my only plan was to find a weapon, something that I could kill him with. I grabbed a knife and walked to my mother's bedroom. I am not sure if she was asleep but I stood in the doorway and told her I was getting ready to kill her husband. My sister was asleep across the hall, so she was trying to get me to be quiet. I refused and told her that she better calls the police because I was going to kill him tonight. I walked into the kitchen with knife and and my mother started yelling at me to stop. She said that the believed me, that it was okay to put the knife down. He was standing in the doorway looking at me with the knife in my hand. That night he confessed to my mother that he had been abusing me, I am not sure if he told her everything. He left that night and I thought that he was gone out of my life forever. I was scared and excited at the possibility that my life would change, with him gone. I actually slept that night and closed my eyes without fear for the first time, I could remember in years. The next afternoon, I was home because my mother did not want me to go to school. He actually came back home, I was shocked and infuriated, and it had been less than twenty-four hours. My mother told me he would get therapy and that he would never touch me again. I told her if he did, she would be a widow because if he came near me again, I would kill him. It was at that moment that I began to hate my mother, to be honest I am not sure if it was really hate. I know that the sight of her made me physically sick and I just did not want to be in her company. The worst part is that I hated myself even more and I knew then that I would kill myself. No one cared about me and the best place for me to be was dead. The next day after school I came home and looked in my secret hiding place for my journals. They were gone, so was every story that I had ever written, every bit of writing that I had saved and produced was gone. I stopped writing after that in fact I stop believing I could write after that. Up until that day I was going to be a lawyer and a writer. I planned to write novels and compound off of my imagination. I looked everywhere for my writing but I could not find it, that was the one thing no one had ever touched and now it was gone. It was mine but that did not matter they took it away from me. I had nothing left and I knew exactly what I needed to do. I think it needs to be said I am not the only one in my family that has accused my step father of abuse. The only difference is the other victim that I know of was silenced by my mother and shamed. She then eventually moved away and I never saw her again. I personally believe that there are more but I don't have evidence of that, so it I speculation.

If you can believe the irony of the situation, they were in the process of adopting a baby at the time this happened. I knew my mother wanted another child and in the background of the abuse she was enduring an unsuccessful quest to have another child. They already had one child together but my mother had faced several complications with that pregnancy and getting pregnant after my sister was born never ended up in a successful pregnancy. She yearned for a son and so they went through the adoption process and successfully obtained a child. I look back now at that time and think that that the grief from miscarriages coupled with her own issues made it impossible for her to protect me. I remember sitting in the library with my mother looking through adoption books thinking that this was insane. My mother was adamant about adopting boy because she wanted a son. Either that or she did not want to bring another victim in the house, I don't know. Eventually the day arrived to go get the baby they were driving into to New York City to pick the baby up. I planned that I would kill myself while they were gone. This new child would make it so no one would miss me anyway. The best thing I could do was disappear, no one really wanted me. My best option was to cease to exist because living with my mother now was unbearable. She was always angry at me for something, it seemed like nothing I did made her happy. I made sure to bring home good grades and to try and excel at everything. I really wanted my mother to be proud of me but she never noticed anything that I did was positive.

I had prepared a letter it was to be my last piece of writing and I addressed it to her stating that my death was the only gift I had to give her. My father raping her made me a daily reminder of her pain. It was like I was her scarlet letter and instead of wearing it on her chest she had to look at me every day. So I would do what should have been done with me in the first place, I was going to kill myself So that day as they prepared to leave, I sat in my room preparing my suicide kit. I was not dressed or ready to go and had verbalized to them several times that I did not want to go. I knew no one would be there to stop me and that no matter what I would succeed that day. I think my mother had an idea that something was going to happen, so she insisted that I go in fact, she order that I go. The ride to New York City was a blur, I remember riding in a hot car because I refused to put my window down. I did not even want to breathe air, they kept commenting that I was afraid to mess up my hair. I remember thinking that they had no clue what really was going to happen. We arrived in New York we pulled up outside of a huge building and went inside to a bland office to see the baby for the first time. The foster mother or the social worker was holding the baby, I am not sure who it was. I do know the woman was trying to give him to my parents but he just kept crying and holding on to her. I just sat there looking at the scene contemplating how I was going to pull my suicide off with them at home. I was just feeling numb like I was already dead. I had to figure out way to carry out my plan because I could not take seeing tomorrow. The woman noticed that I had not attempted to pick him up and asked me to give it a try. I walked over to him and he reached his arms out to me and my heart melted. He hung on to me like his life depended on it and at that moment he gave me a reason to live once again. The ride home was so amazing he sat next to me in the car and held on to my finger tightly. I was his connection to the world and he needed me. I was so excited I wanted to stay home the next few days to help with him but my mother said that he needed to get used to her. It seemed like because of that moment she tried to keep me away from him. After that day my stepfather never touch me sexually again but the mental and financial abuse remained a part of my life. I tried that year to kill myself several times, it never worked and no one even noticed. I remember one day I drank almost an entire bottle of Nyquil, I woke up the next evening and no one even mentioned it to me. As an adult I spend a tremendous amount of time reflecting on my childhood. Reflecting not because I don't want to forget. Reflecting because I want my children to have a better one than I did. As Mother's Day approaches, I look at my children and I have hope. I hope than when they are my age, they will look back in love at our relationship. Mothers day for me is a battle. Should I call her and pretend that, the years of abuse she ignored don't matter anymore? Should I call her and say thank you for having me? For having me even though I am a constant reminder of your rapist? My mothers husband was never punished for his crimes according to the law. I left and he was able to resume life. To stay with his family and pretend that he was father of the year. I lived with the pain, guilt and regret. I loved my siblings an I did not want them to loose their father. I knew that he abused me because I was not his child. I grew up without a father and with a mother that I felt hated me. As an adult I look back and realize that I was a constant reminder of her rape. What I can't understand is, if she knew that pain. I mean if she knew that pain, why would she let me suffer, the same. Then allow me to live in a daily hell, of seeing my abuser. It is almost like, if she was going to suffer than I should suffer. I never choose my life and as a teen wanted to end my life. I am thankful that I had the foresight to see a better future for myself. To see living and a better future for myself. I am at point in my life where I need to make some decisions. I can't be silent anymore I have learned this is not my secret to keep. I realized now that my mother chose my stepfather and the appearance of normality over me. I have yet to accept it and I am not sure if it is the source of the agony that I carry in my heart will ever disappear. I also know that I am the source of her agony, a child of rape. It must be difficult to see the product of violence everyday of your life. I can't imagine what it may feel like to violated like that and have a child as a result of it.

I laugh out loud at people who say abortion is never an option, they must not be a child of rape. I know my life has value and all that jazz, I am not suicidal and writing my last words. It is just that there is insurmountable pain in knowing that you are the product of your mother's greatest pain, that is difficult for her to love you. When I think of the horrible and nasty things she did to me in my life, I can only think that is why. To allow you child to suffer repeatedly the same pain you had endured, in order to keep a man. To save face, seems just cruel and inhumane. It was torture to have to look at his face everyday and even after I left their home. He was still a part of my life, to visit my mother meant to visit him. To call meant he might answer the phone. She wanted me to act like nothing happened and pretend. It was taking me under, on the outside I was a highly functioning educated woman. On the inside, I was eating my self to death and in constant pain.

I made the hardest decision, I had to make in my life. I let her go and separated myself from her and my siblings. My little sister knows and thinks I am a liar; he is her father. My little brother does not know and I have no idea what they have told him. I doubt my mother will ever own up to it and tell them. They are all that she has. So my family is my husband and children, that is who I have. Other family members exist but they are not really a daily part of my life. I can't lie, I miss my mother! There was a time before my sister was born; I think I was seven. That I remember walking with her and talking with her, I felt her love. After my sister was born things changed, she was critically ill. She had to be the center of attention and I felt lost. My sister eventually recovered but that attention on her remained. Not really an abnormal situation except because of that my stepfather was allowed to victimize me.

THE RUIN

It felt like my mother hated me and no matter what I did it did not seem that she was ever going to love me like she did my sister. When I graduated from high school and got into a private university, she seemed happy to everyone else but never smiled at me. There was no party or celebration just the silence that existed in my home knowing I was leaving. She seemed excited that I was leaving but really did not want to do anything to help me prepare. I was working, to be clear I had been working since I was thirteen years old, she had changed one of the numbers on my working papers so I could start working a year earlier than I was supposed to. My senior year of high school, I met a new boy who I managed to keep away from my abuser. I lived off the fact that I was going to leave the people behind that were causing me all the pain. Since I was dating a boy from another school, I was going to two proms. My mother said she would only help me purchase one dress. So I would have to find the second one on my own. That seems reasonable considering I was working but the reality is most of the money I earned she borrowed or I would spend to help put food in the house. I finally had purchased my self a television from local rental place and I was paying for that every week as well. She seemed kind of disgusted with my prom situation anyway so I knew she really was not going to help me out. My stepfather purchased the prom dress from a local consignment store that all the girls in my area shopped at for prom. The second prom dress I stole from a local department store because I did not have the money to buy one. Other than the dress, my hair shoes everything else I had to furnish for my self. There was no limo or fancy car but I went to both proms. I remember each night because I felt beautiful both times and I could not remember feeling beautiful before. At my prom I remember walking through the door and it seemed like some of the people I went to school with saw me for the first time. It sounds like a scene out of an eighties movie, I know but for me at that time it was real. By the time graduation rolled around my mother received a settlement from social security administration. She had started getting injured at work repeatedly and eventually a doctor said her health was too poor to work. Which meant that financially we were suffering. The money from my job was used get groceries. My mother came up with the idea that she could come through my line at my job and that I would either not scan the groceries of use fake coupons on them. My job helped provided necessary funds that we needed to survive. She actually even convinced one of the friends I was working with to do it too, that way I was not the only line she could go through. I quit that job and started working at another store across town because I knew she was going to get me arrested before I could go to college. She actually ended up getting the other girl in trouble because when I left and got the other job she was not able to run her scam at the new store. I did some things that I was not proud of because I thought that I had to do them so we could survive. I was kid who thought that if I could anything to make my mother happy, I should do it.

The summer I was to start college I turned eighteen, so social security sent me a check in my name. I am not sure of the amount of money that my mother received but it was over ten thousand dollars. She actually was able to put five thousand dollars down to lease a SUV. When the check came in the mail with my name on it, I was not even aware it was coming and I was shocked. I actually got exited because I was heading off to college and saw the money as an opportunity to help me with school. As quickly as that thought came, she was pouncing on me like a rabbit animal. I was still standing on the porch at the mailbox when she came out side and told me the check was not mine and that I had to sign it over to her because it was her money anyway. She said they only sent it in my name and they should not have because it is her money not mine. I was not a fool but I did not fight with her, I knew that she would make me miserable until I gave it her. We had been in this position with money before and no matter how much I had she always found a way to get some of it. Eventually before I left for summer college they took me and spent a couple of hundred dollars at the mall. I am not trying to minimalize that act of spending a few hundred dollars on me for summer close. However, living in upstate New York, the weather requires that you have winter clothing. Snow and cold weather is guaranteed and shorts would not be useful once fall came. I used to be mad at myself about that shopping trip because I thought I should have been more realistic. I should have purchased only what I knew I needed. In my mind at that time I was just so excited to shop that I purchased items that a teen age girl would

When the fall semester approached and winter was upon us, I saw my mother driving past campus. I caught up with her and she was heading into a specialty shoe store next to the college campus with my little sister. They were purchasing a few pair of boots for my sister and I made the mistake of thinking that she might purchase me pair too. She got an attitude with me just for asking her for anything and I left the store. I was going to school in upstate New York and I had to walk across campus in the snow without any boots.

I decided at that moment that I would try my best to never ask her for anything again. She on the other hand knew when I got my student loan refunds and always seemed to need something around that time. It seemed like the only time she would call me was to ask for money. I just could not understand it she had just received a major settlement but she always needed my money. Let me say at this point that my mother did make sure certain thing happened for me. She did not totally abandon me but what she gave me never equaled what she took from me. I would always give to her because I just did not know how to tell her no. Eventually I decide to try and get a credit card like all the other kids on campus and I was denied. I did not understand how that was possible because I had never purchased anything on credit. I ordered my credit report and found that I was tens of thousands of dollars in debt. Most of the debts were incurred before I was legally able to purchase anything on credit. I was devastated; I could not even get a cell phone. No one would extend me credit, so I went to see the campus attorney. We went through the credit report and called the companies to get address information and contact information for the accounts. It turned out they all belong to my mother or my aunt. My mother had placed phone bills and electricity bills in my name. Not just at our own home but in order to get service in apartments for my aunt. These electric bills were thousands of dollars and there were too many of them to count. He was able to get some them removed based on the statute of limitations but most them remained. I was told that I would have to file a police report and press charged against my mother to get them removed from my credit report.

I remember sitting in the lawyer's office and bawling because I knew that I could not press charges against my mother. I would have to wait seven years or find a way to get what I needed without credit. The reality is that living without credit is very difficult in this world. When I called my mother to tell her what I found out about my credit report all I got was silence. I don't think I heard from her for a month after that. I already had a job but I picked up two more-part time jobs, to pay for books and other expenses. The summer after my Freshman year I worked on campus and was able to buy myself a car. The car was registered and insured in my mother name or so I thought. That winter I was driving with my boyfriend and backed into a parked car. I provided the woman with my insurance information and apologized profusely. With in days I received a letter stating that I was responsible for he damages because I had no insurance. I don't remember who this woman was but I remember going to her house to apologize and explain that I did not know there was no insurance on the car. I had been giving my mother money for insurance monthly. So I never worried about insurance I just assumed I had it. This woman told me that she was not going to sue me because in the bible it says that it would wrong for her to do so. My car was not damaged it was an old jeep with a metal frame. Luckily I was spared and until this day when I see someone I need I think of that woman. So I give when I can and sometimes when I can't.

After the accident the next time I heard from my mother was to ask me to help with money for groceries because they needed food. She always called me with a desperate story, no lights, water or food. She picked me up and we went to the grocery store and purchased over two hundred dollars in groceries. I went to write a check from one of my accounts and they declined it. I did not understand why but they gave me number to call and see why. I ended up using the money I had in my pocket to pay for the groceries. My mother stood next to me looking just as shocked as I did about the check declining. The next day I called the number and they stated that I had some bad checks floating around out there. When the company sent me copies of the check, without a doubt it was my mother's handwriting on the check. I did not even call her ask about it, I just made arrangements to pay the checks, so that I would not go to jail.

My financial situation put me in a lonely place; the people around me were taking trips and going on spring break vacations. I could only afford to live day to day and survive. I had an acquaintance that would always ask me why I did not have a cell phone. I was kind embarrassed to explain the situation to her so I lied and said I only had one for emergencies. Well unfortunately that lie came back to haunt me one day when we were all in my car driving to buffalo and the car broke down. I was not really a party girl but I was excited to make a road trip to another school to go to a party with girls who I thought at the time were prettier and better than me. I had to to admit when the car broke down that I did not have a phone. So I had to walk to a pay phone and call home. We were close to Rochester so The same brother that took me on the first trip to Rochester came and picked me and all the girls up. We stayed at their house over night and then they brought us back to campus. My car was towed away and my parents said they would take care of it for me. I left the following week for Spain and I never saw it again, I know that it was not the end of the world but the humiliation, just contributed to the isolation that I lived in. I really never wanted to see that girl again and so I stopped really hanging out with them and moved off campus when I got back from Spain. My tuition was paid due to scholarship and through the tuition assistance that I received because my stepfather worked at the university. However, going to private institution and housing, fees and books ran almost ten thousand dollars a year. When I decided to spend some time studying in Spain. I was shocked because they went out of their way to help me pay for my plane ticket. When I returned they had a party for me with all of our family in the back yard. To top it all off they had bought me another car. I really felt at that party that my mother cared about me and that she decided to show me and everyone else. Until after the party, they told me that I could not keep they car. They needed the money from the car to pay some bills. This was not the first time this had happened, I could recount countless birthdays and holidays where I was given gifts that had to be returned. The worst cases were when they would tell they would get me after a holiday because they only had money for the little kids. That the little kids would not understand missing Christmas. To be honest I heard we would get you after a birthday or holiday so many times that I never expected them to get me anything. I would just wait and see what my Grandmother would give me instead. I eventually learned that my grandmother gave them the money for the car. The fact that my Grandmother would buy me things would piss my mother off. I overheard countless conversations where she talked about my grandmother buying me things and that she did too much for me and not enough for my sister. I was so conditioned to this treatment that I used to think it was just what how my life was. That I was not worthy of much of anything and I spent all my time trying to help everyone else succeed. I truly felt that I had no value in this world and I just accepted a lot of things in my life that I should not have.

The worst part of this situation was seeing him every day, even though I was in college, that was where he worked. It was like I had to relive the experiences over and over again. After I left home I tried my best not to come back. When I did, I would feel horrible for days afterward. It was like I would have a dark cloud following me after a visit home. I was in luck because they rarely visited me and would never let me take my sister or brother anywhere. I had a long conversation with my little sister few years ago in which she informed me that many people in her life have no idea that she has a big sister. When she told me that, it broke my heart,

I left my family to escape the pain of seeing my abuser daily. As a result, my sister and brother have no idea who I really am. My mother never showed for a family day or any events at the university. It was like they were afraid I would tarnish them in some way. The reality is that I loved my siblings so much that I had decided a long time ago not to tell them what happened. I did not want them to suffer on my account; I could not bear them hating me. It never made a difference; my siblings had no idea who I was because I was never around. There is an eight year and seventeen-year age difference between us. We spent no time together and they always seemed suspicious of me. I am not sure why but I assume, there were not many positive things said about me when I was not around. I was an outsider, in complete and total exile it seemed. I know now that the life I was living was insane and abnormal. To me it just seemed like the life I was dealt and I had to make the best of it.

THE REACTION

Around the same time that I turned twelve years old, I started to see that my body was changing. It scared me a little because I did not want my stepfather to notice me. I remember walking down the street in a bright yellow sweat suit after school one day. Some neighborhood guys were yelling catcalls at me; remember I was only twelve years old. Comments like "what is your mamma feeding you with all that ass?". The idea of other men noticing me was stressful because I already had one mans unwanted attention.

It actually made me not want to really go outside, the fear of men noticing my body. I was stressed all the time, wondering if they were looking at me. Wondering what they would do to me. In my mind the possibility of them hurting me was very real considering what was happening to me at home. Food became my medicine, when I was upset I would find myself in the kitchen eating. As a result, I gained weight and I knew that I was fat. Everyone else knew that I was fat too; the kids at school were cruel and told me I was fat all the time. Going to the doctor sucked because every year he would tell me that I was overweight and that I needed to lose weight. After those appointments my mother would tell me I was just big boned. My stepfather however would call me nick names like fridge and big. He would call me those things instead of my name all the time. My mother never corrected him; it was like she thought they were appropriate nicknames for a young girl.

My weight was a problem in all aspects of my life, we were a sedentary family, and so I did not play sports and do any type of activity. In fact, we ate horribly too and in reality everyone in my house was obese with the exception of my little sister and brother. Our beverage of choice was soda and we drank it like it was water. In fact, I don't think that I even drank water unless I was in school. We rarely have a variety of food and basically ate fried food and butter heavy starchy vegetables. Most of my family saw me as a target for jokes about my weight. One of my cousins would joke about my weight every single time he saw me. I am sure that I heard the phrase: you would be so pretty if you lost some weight, once a day.

By the time I was in high school, my weight made me feel like I was undesirable. I was the fat girl and I did not fit in. The funny thing is that I had never really been on the scale and I did not know how much I weighed. When looking back at my medical records, I saw that I weighed 179 pounds and basically stayed that weight throughout high school. I was and am 5'3, so clinically I was considered obese but in reality I was not as overweight as I felt at the time.

I was under the impression that my weight was the reason I was unhappy in life. So if I just lost the weight that my life would be better and I would be happy. The truth is that I have had an eating disorder for most of my life. I started off as a binge eater, progressed into bulimia, dabbled in anorexia and then returned to my friend bulimia to keep me sane. My life resolved around food, what I could eat and what I could not eat. Food defined my moods and if I felt particularly fat that day then my life was horrible. If I got on the scale and the number was pleasing, then I was happy again. Before I began thinking about losing weight I was a binge eater and I would eat any and everything that I could find. For me the food was like a drug it gave me a high that would last for a while then it would disappear and I would need to eat again to make me feel better. Binge eating is something that you do in private, so I require a certain amount of isolation. So I would eat with people and then sneak off to consume large amounts of food in private. My portions were always huge and it seemed like sometimes I could not understand that my body was was full until I was tired.

While I was in high school it seemed that I could not connect with my peers, I once again an outsider. Lunch was the worst time of day, I did not want people to see me eat and I did not really have a crowd that I fit in. I would just just cling on to a group and sort of be a part of it, usually they were nice girls who would include me. The problem was they were real friends and eventually I would feel like an outsider in that group too. They were thin in my eyes and I was fat, so they were better than I was. Which made them beautiful and me ugly so I felt like I was not worth much of anything. Everyone I knew was moving on but I was trapped in this place that was consumed by what my body looked like. I was a very good actress and most of the time I never let on that I felt inferior or uglier that the people I was around. The fact is that before I met my husband I had never been bowling, to bonfire, any restaurant that was not a fast food restaurant except Red Lobster. I only attended two school dances and one of them was the prom. I was rarely invited to attend parties or to go skating. My life revolved around a secret and nothing else could fit into my world. So the only the only thing I had was food, it was my friend and confidant. Food was also my enemy and my drug at the same time, everything I did revolved around food or when I was going to eat.

The reality is that Edith (my eating disorder) has been in control of my life for as long I can remember. She arrived very early in my life as a child and remained the only thing that I could rely on to remain constant in my life. She was a mechanism to control my anxiety and the panic state that my body remained in on daily basis. I was having on average three to four panic attacks a day from the time I was in the second grade. The panic attacks made it impossible for me to deal with people in groups. So I began to isolate myself from others, withdrawing from the few groups that I used to belong to. I did not want anyone to see me when I was having a panic attack, I had one in elementary school once and I really did not know what was happening to me because it appeared that I was sitting in class and just lost me breathe. So I started hyperventilating at my desk and grabbing at my throat, I could feel the tears falling down my face. I really thought I was dying and no one was there to help me. Children can be cruel and many of them made fun of me for it, which made me so angry that I could not contain myself. I believe I actually threw a desk at another student that day. As a result of the experience I would have a panic attack sitting next to someone and they would have no idea what I was going through. It would just appear as if I focusing on something else or not paying attention to them.

Let me be clear if you have never had a panic attack then you really need to understand what was happening to my body. My chest would tighten and it would fell like I could not breathe, like I was in constant state of holding my breath. I could feel the tears brimming at my eyes but I would never let them fall in front of other people. These attacks would happen without warning and frequently on daily basis. Many times I would burst out in tears during situations because I could not contain the panic attack. Many people in my family saw me a cry baby because of those outbursts. My cure, the medicine I chose was food and it worked. I would be in panic mode and start a binge and by the end of the binge the attack would be over. I would feel better than I did before the attack. There is always catch and as I binged more to get through panic attacks, I gained more weight. By the time I was at the end of my freshman year of college, I was clinically obese.

I remember going to see one of my acquaintances that summer and expressing to her how I felt about my weight gain. We were standing in the street in front of her house at that time. She seemed like she cared and was concerned about me. Later I learned that next day that she had told some of the other people we knew that I was fatter than ever before. Although this person was not important part of my life those comments helped Edith to further take over my life. I decided that I was going to lose weight and show those people that I was worthy. To prove that I was beautiful to world, in my mind I thought that would solve all of my problems. So I would binge to get rid of my anxiety and stop the panic attacks but when I was full, I would purge all the food out of my system. It got to the point where I would purge after every meal and nothing seemed worthy of staying in my system. I would feel guilty about having anything left in my system that might make me gain weight. While I was away in Spain, I perfected the cycle of my eating disorder. As a result, I came home about forty pounds lighter. When I got off the plane my family made such a big deal about the weight loss. That was all anyone could talk about was how much weight I had lost. It seemed like I was acceptable in the eye of others having lost that weight. So I set goals for myself to lose more. I would run every single morning as long and far as I could get getting up to about 7 miles a day. Missing a workout was not an option. Hunger was not part of my life and was feeling that I did not want to acknowledge. When it came to food there were only food I could not eat and foods that were acceptable to remain in my body until I could purge.

When I met my husband a lot of things changed in my life, he was different and for a while I left Edith behind to be with him. It only lasted for a short while, if you consider how long I had been in a relationship Edith. So I once again gained weight but It was seen as happy relationship weight. By the time we got engaged I was once again obese and binge eating to reduce my anxiety and panic attacks. My husband did not learn about my panic and anxiety until we had been married 11 years. We planned our wedding and decided that it was going to take place in less than 7 months from our engagement. I went to a weight loss center and learned some new tricks to help Edith take over my life. It resulted in an eighty-pound weight loss and I still felt I was too fat on my wedding day. In fact, I remember sitting at the table during my wedding afraid to even eat the meal that was served to me at the reception. I was married and I had a man who loved me but I was not even sure that was real. I doubted it and I thought that he would leave at any moment. So I never really thought my feeling were valid in our relationship. I was flawed and he was not.

Although he knew about my sexual abuse, he still treated me like a normal person. He never let my stepfather influence him and it is my belief that they don't like him until this day because he was unable to influenced. I thought that our marriage would be based on what I looked like, so if I gained weight I would try and be the best wife I could be, always giving in no matter what the circumstances was. I was a doormat and I lived in constant fear that he would look at me one day and see that I was not what he wanted. That he made a mistake and I was ugly, fat and broken.

Edith told me that I needed to get my shit together. That meant that I needed to get my weight under control but before I knew it I was pregnant with my first child. This was an excuse to eat and eat and eat. That is what I did and I gained the eighty pounds plus more back by the time I had my first child. After having my son, I was told that I needed to have my second child as soon as possible.

I did not head that warning but instead of trying to have a baby I was back into my cycle of the binge and purge in between mommy duties. The sad part was that I was breast feeding so the weight loss that I enjoyed in the past from the binge and purge was no longer effective. I had to eat in order for my milk supply to be sufficient for my baby to thrive. He was more important than my need to feel worthy or beautiful, so while I was nursing my son I gave up the binge and purge so that he could be healthy. Edith did not leave me alone though. I agonized through every bite of food that I ate. It was like I was ingesting poison into my body and I could feel each pound as it grew on my body. In my adult life was consumed with my appearance, if I had to be fat then my hair, nails and makeup needed to be flawless. So that at least I could say I was a fashionable fat girl. I hated the mirror and looking in it could bring me to tears or a panic attack. I am not sure which was worse to be honest because both them seemed like a burden that I did not want to bear. After successfully getting pregnant and having my second child Edith took over my life again. While I was pregnant the doctor made me go see a heart specialist because of an irregular heart rhythm that was noticed during a routine prenatal checkup. I remember going to the doctor after having the tests performed and sitting in the waiting room rubbing my belly. When I was called back into the doctor's office he basically told me that all my test was clear. The only thing that was wrong with me was that I was fat and if I wanted to die then keep eating myself to death. So I knew that as soon as I had my baby I had to do something to change my life. Changing my life meant losing weight and that is when Edith began to run the show.

I don't think when I started my plan I was an all out attempt to dive head first into my eating disorder, to be honest I really did not even acknowledge that I had an eating disorder at that time. After my sun was born I joined a weight loss group at work. I was breast feeding but also providing him with formula to supplement. The weight started to fall off and I started to work harder to make sure it did not not come back. I was once again running everyday and sometimes I either ran to or from work. In addition to my diet anytime I had what I would considered a cheat meal I would purge because I could not let anything stop my progress. In addition to running I was doing two work out DVD's a day, on in the morning and one at night. My husband was working evenings so he had no idea how much I was working out. On his days off he would say that I was going too hard but I would not listen to him. I was out of control and I did not see a way to stop, I was a roll and within 6 months of having my son I had lost a hundred pounds. I was running races and entering different weight loss competitions.

I was a part of anything that would promote healthy eating or weight loss. I went so far as to start a blog and a Facebook page to track my progress. Everyone knew what I was doing and it made people pay attention to me. I would receive messages from other women and old classmates asking me how I was able to lose the weight. It felt good to have a secret to successful weight loss and to be a symbol of something positive. Eventually I earned spot in a weight loss magazine and was I was able to travel to New York City and do a photo shoot. I was on the most amazing high that I had ever been on. Behind all of that I was in pain, the constant running and working out was causing me joint pain but I was ignoring it. My biggest fear was getting fat again, so the saying "No Pain, No Gain" was a motto I lived by. When the contract at the local community college I was working at came to an end. We had to move across the country in order for me to take another teaching job. Moving from a major to city to a suburban city provided so major challenges for my workout routine. I was no longer able to walk out of my house and hit the pavement for a five mile run, there were no sidewalks. I had to join a gym and find away to make up for the miles I was missing. So I found a workout out program and joined a gym. I would be in the gym for about two to three hours in order to complete my routine five days a week. As far as I was concerned there was never a reason to miss a workout. My husband started to notice that the amount of weight I was losing was alarming and he even commented that I was losing to much weight. I took that as a compliment and was outraged he thought that could be a problem. Unfortunately for Edith my body decided that it was unable to sustain the rate of pressure that I was putting it through. It came to a point where I was unable to run, my ankles and knees would not allow me to run. I would still try but the pain would be so intense that I would not get far. I thought It would be an easy fix so I went to the doctor and was sent to a specialist. After several X rays and a MRI, I was told that I had arthritis. There is no cure and it was recommended that I start doing more low impact exercises. The fact that I was unable to run, began to eat at me. It was like something was stolen from me. I was using running to replace the food to get rid of my panic attacks. So not being able to run meant I had to return to food. Food meant that I would gain weight, gaining weight meant I would be fat. My life was spinning out of control and the only thing I could think of was to go to the gym. I remember the moment it all hit the fan. I was sitting at my desk looking in the mirror, I could see my children and husband cuddled up on the couch. I however, was sitting at the desk in full panic attack mode as I prepared to go to the gym. At that moment it hit me that I could no longer live this life. Either I needed to end my life or find a way to stop this cycle I was in. Looking at my children and my husband I knew that I had to live. So instead of going the the gym, I began to google my symptoms and found a treatment center near me. The very next day without my husband's knowledge I went to meet with an admission counselor at the treatment center. I was informed at that time that I would need to enter into inpatient or intensive day treatment program. I was kind of shocked that I was in such a state that I would need to go in to an inpatient treatment program. What I did know was that I was tired of living my life through such skewed lenses. I went home and told my husband that I had to go to treatment.

He was shocked and angry at the same time. He was however adamant that no matter what the cost or time needed that I follow through with going to recovery. Spent four months in an intensive day treatment program then two months in an evening outpatient treatment program. I learned that I was not about food, what I looked like, or who thought I was intelligent. The reality was I was depressed, suffering from PTSD and I needed to get help. Recovery saved my life and as I sit here today having been panic attack free all day. I know that it was all worth it, every minute and every dollar. The thing about recovery is that while you are going through it there are so many highs and lows and it is not until the end that you feel like you're on a level playing field. You see your self through so many different eyes and realized that you have not really been living. You'd been pretending this entire time. You began to learn things about yourself. It amazes you that you are stronger than you thought you were. That weakness you thought was helping to holding you back was strength the entire time. You made it through a situation that not many people could survive. You begin to actually see your self, not the bad thoughts you had about yourself. You really see who you are and it is beautiful, nothing short of amazing to wake up after a lifetime of blindness. The thing about recovery is that in my opinion it is never over. I can always catch myself reverting back to old habits or listening to that destructive inner voice. Then I have to go back to basics and look in the mirror and remember that I can see myself now. That seeing myself is worth ignoring the voice that tells me I am not worth it. That's what works for me and I am not physician so I can not say what will work for you. However, I bet if you take some time to stare in the mirror and really see your self. Not your imperfections but the amazingness that is simply you. It will make a difference and I will not lie to you and say it will be easy. It's not easy and everyday it takes work; some days it just takes more than others.

THE HEARBREAK

The truth of it is that I was never planning to have children. In my mind I was going to become a lawyer and travel the world. Children did not seem to fit into that plan and so when I entered the world of infertility my whole life changed. I was living what many may say a carefree, childfree life when a bomb was dropped into my lap. I had gone for a routine gynecological appointment which at the time did not seem important. I was on birth control and I was really not thinking about pregnancy or children. One day while sitting on my old tattered couch, my phone rang and my life changed. The nurse from my doctor's office called and said they had been trying to reach me since my last appointment. I was shocked and thought that maybe I forget to pay copay or something. She explained that my bloodwork came back that I was pregnant and that I should come in as soon as possible to be seen. I was numb and floored, me of all people pregnant. I could not see myself having children or being someone's baby mama for that matter. I was in for a rude awakening because as soon as I hung up the phone I felt a warm gush. I looked down and saw that my entire lap was covered in blood. I was not sure what was happening but I ran to the bathroom and I was stood in the shower as blood just poured from my body. I cleaned myself up and called the doctor where I was informed that it was possible I was having a miscarriage. So I slowly dressed and went to the doctor where they confirmed that I was in deed having a miscarriage. From that moment my life changed, the reality of being pregnant and not having a choice if I wanted to be or not was heartbreaking. It seemed like my focus immediately changed to wanting a baby and I did not really care if anyone liked it or not. I joined an online website and started doing research online about getting pregnant. The fact is that up until that point I had no real idea how my body worked. So I immersed myself information about fertility. I started to learn about how my body worked, ovulation, cervical mucus and the when I could get pregnant. I purchased ovulation tests and pregnancy tests in bulk through online vendors. I would chat online with other women who were trying to have babies and find out new information it was like I had found a new community to become a part of. Eventually I was pregnant again but just like the first time as soon as I found out it ended with a gush of blood in my pants. This time I was at work when it occurred and I had to be rushed to the hospital by ambulance. It was determined at that time that I had fibroids and that my right tube was damaged. I had to undergo laparoscopic surgery where it was determined that the fibroid would prevent them from repairing my tube with out actually opening up my stomach. This was a pivotal moment for me because the doctor actually cut me open, saw a fibroid the size of a twelve-week old fetus and left it there. He repaired the tube completed the Dilation and cartilage to remove the fetus and closed me up. He told me that the Fibroid had nothing to do with my miscarriage and I believed him. As a young black woman with great healthcare insurance who was seeing one of the best doctors in the area, I had no reason to doubt him. The reality is that he was not telling the truth, the fibroid was the problem and as long as it remained in my uterus I would continue to have miscarriages. I have my suspicions why he lied to me but since I decided that I telling my truth I am going to tell what I feel. That doctor was used to seeing uneducated black girls walk through the door and helping them get pregnant was not his goal. He saw them as a drain on the system and he never took the time to see me as a person. I was just another black girl and if I could never carry a baby to term the world would be a batter place. Once I learned about the fibroid I started to do some research and slowly it became clear that this doctor did not have my best interest in mind. Right around this time we moved to another state and I sought out another doctors. Upon my first visit she was mortified and wanted to send me down for surgery immediately. She told me that she could not understand how I was still walking around. This woman, this doctor not only made is possible for me to have children but she saved my life. After having the fibroid removed I was pregnant with in 6 months. Her advice was for me to go ahead and try to have another baby immediately because the fibroids would return. The location that they were growing in would make it impossible for and egg to implant in my uterus and survive. I was young and dumb, so I did not listen to her. Having one at that time seemed like enough and I would worry about another one at a later date. Right around the time my son was one, we decided it was time to have another baby. So I jumped off the birth boards and back to the trying to conceive band wagon. I purchased fertility monitors, monitored my temperature and cervical mucus. Nothing was happening and after a year I knew the doctor was right. So we headed to the fertility specialist. Going to the fertility specialist is very daunting especially when you are considered young. In my mind I felt like less than a woman, here was another thing in my life that showed I was worthless. Giving my husband a child was supposed to be easy. It was something that I should be able to do with out spending tons of money and time on medication and testing. That in fact was my reality so I dove into it. I started taking fertility medications and having inter uterine inseminations(IUI). We found out during my first and very painful insemination that my cervix was blocked with scar tissue, it could have been from the first surgery to repair my tube, the myomectomy to remove the fibroid or the C-section to have my son. The doctor could not tell but he knew that IUI's were the least effective way for me to get pregnant. I would need to undergo inviter fertilization(IVF) to get pregnant but my insurance at the time did not cover it, so we pushed on with the IUI's. Over the next three years I had three more miscarriages. Each one chipped away at my ability to feel like a woman, the worthlessness seemed to cling in the air. Everyone around me would said just wait, your stressing about it too much. It will just happen if you don't think about it. LIES, they had no idea that I would not get pregnant waiting or reducing my stress level. The only way I would get pregnant would be medical intervention. The forth year we were trying t conceive our second child, we moved to another state and my insurance covered IVF. I once again did my research and found the best doctor within in 3 hours and began the quest to have another baby. I was so focused during this process that I did not see my husband, he was tired and frustrated with the process but I was on quest to have another child and prove I was woman. We started the first round of IVF in September and transferred two embryos, I fond out on Thanksgiving that it did not work. My husband had enough and he wanted to wait to try again but the doctor said they had one embryo left and it was perfect. All I had to do was keep injecting the medication and they could thaw and do a six-day transfer. I convinced my husband to push ahead and the frozen embryo transfer(FET) was a success. I was pregnant but I was also afraid that a miscarriage would end this pregnancy too. So I obsessed over every symptom and any sign of complication I was at the doctor. I was horrible to live with and my husband is indeed the best man I know for holding me up during that time. That summer I gave birth to another little boy, who looked just like his father. He was my gift and I knew that was all I was going to get. IVF is a very difficult process to go through, shots three times a day and oral medications. Constant sonograms and the waiting is just unbearable. I knew mentally I could never go through that process again and mentally survive. So we decided that we would just be happy with two children. Shortly after giving birth I stumbled across a veteran IVF board it brought back for me the struggle. I remember reading infertility blogs that turned into baby blogs and feeling a bit sad. I was always happy to see the conversion but still a bit sad that I was still blogging through the same battle. Reading through the pain those ladies are going through brought me back. I hoped that my blog was not causing that specific pain for anyone. Infertility is one the tabooest and least discussed illness in the world. We usually suffer in silence and have few people in real life to relate to. This has been a life long struggle for me. I was 30 years old and veteran in fertility world because of the issues I was dealing with early in my life. The dedication to having children has taken eight years out of my life. With the conception of my last child came the realization that his birth would end my trying to conceive journey. If a third child came into our family, it would be due to an unplanned unexpected pregnancy. Which for me is was not likely to happen but most likely due to the adoption of and older African American child.

Before we knew it we were moving to yet another state for my career. Moving to where we hoped would the last state move we would make and finally settle down. My youngest had just turned two and my husband approached me. He said let's try without trying, no medical intervention, let's see if it just happens. I had lost a ton of weight and my fibroids were so small the could not really even be seen during my sonograms. So even though I was unsure, I agreed what could it hurt. To be honest we had fun and did not think about the consequences.

March of that year I found out that my father died and that I needed to bury him. I was crushed and rushed back home to settle his affairs. When I got back I was grieving and a light period was passed off as stress. In my mind I knew exactly what it was but I refused to talk about it or grieve another loss. I acted like it just never happened and tried to keep moving. The fall was quickly approaching and I missed my period. I panicked immediately because I knew that I had to have medical intervention immediately to carry this baby. I was in a panic and I called the doctor I was seeing in the are but the receptionist refused to make an appointment until I was farther along. I ended up calling around to several different doctors to get an appointment explaining my issue. Finally, I was able to get into see a doctor who prescribed the progesterone that I needed. One of the reasons that I had so many miscarriages is that I also had luteal phase defect. Which basically means that my body did not naturally produce enough progesterone to sustain a pregnancy. I was not hopeful about tis pregnancy but my husband was elated, we have finally did it. This was going to be his girl, I started cramping the week before Christmas and I was in intense pain. I passed out in the kitchen and we ended up in the emergency room. Which actually just resulted in a large bill to pay and no real information. They could not ell me what was wrong and basically told me I had to wait. I knew it was over but I put on a brave face and made sure that my family had a great Christmas. The day after Christmas we went to the doctor and he was able to preform a D&C right in the office. I could see in my husbands face that he was devastated and scared all at the same time. The doctor asked us before we left the office that day. What we were going to do to prevent this from happening again. He said it was not likely that I would carry a baby to term and we would be in this situation again. I was so angry that he chose that time to make that statement. I had just sat in an examination room and lost what I thought was my daughter. My husband was so angry with me because he knew that I sat through the holiday and suffered in silence. He knew that I was in pain the whole time and did not tell him. He vowed that I would never have to go through that pain every again. Within the next few months he has a vasectomy guaranteeing that I would never have to suffer another miscarriage again. His sacrifice will never be forgotten. There is so much pain that I have gone through that he could do nothing about but he knew what he could control and he made sure to handle that situation so I would not have to. I can't say that I don't yearn for more children but I look at the two miracles that I gave birth to and I know that I a blessed. We are not all able to get pregnant easy or carry babies to term. Unless you have been in the shoes of a woman that has dealt with infertility or multiple pregnancy loss then you have no idea the pain that it causes. I just hope the next time you meet someone trying to get pregnant or has lost a child, you choose your words wisely. Sometimes if you don't understand the best thing you can do is be quiet and spare them the pain of your ignorance. Along my journey I met some very incompetent medical professionals and my lack of knowledge at the time kept me in the dark. The best thing we can do for our children is teach them about their bodies and make sure they understand what they can do. Give them a voice and allow them to use it when they feel like something is not right. I know that the person I am now I would not have accepted that doctor leaving me in the condition I was in. I would have used my voice but back then I did not even know I had one. Silence about trauma does not just affect one area of our life, it spreads and it becomes a part of who you are. As I get older and look at my boys and I have to ask my self a question? How will they survive in this world with out extended family? If by chance something was to happen to us, we honestly have not one person we would trust with our children. Now that is scary to me.

Why would this be on my mind right now? I guess because after all the pain and grief we went through to bring these children in the world, I am now aware that I am not able to give them the blood family they deserve. That is scary they have only a few people who really know who they are. So now we have to create a family for them that is safe and will provide then with the people they will need in their lives. To be happy children who can navigate this scary world. We are in a new city once again and I feel the loneliness creeping up in my soul. It is hard to make new connections sometimes. I am keeping my self open to new people. I long for the big family dinners of past. With loud people, tons of good food and most of all family. Regardless of what was going on when "Mommy" (my grandmother) was alive we all came together. Played spades, ate and congregated. I was not aware of her powerful pull at the time. Now in her absence I realize what exactly a matriarch is and what the role consists of. My family situation is because of sexual abuse and fragmented parental relationships. Neither of which I can control. I guess part of the residual pain of being a survivor of sexual abuse is that separation occurs. Not because you want to be separated but because it is the only way to remain healthy. I look at my absentee father and sexual abuse accommodating mother and wish I had a solvable family problem. I yearn for simplicity because choosing to spend Christmas with my mother, brother and sister includes spending Christmas with the man who abused me for 10 years. Spending Christmas with my father, would mean finding him first, then figuring out if he knows who I am and finally asking if I am welcome. I just miss my Grandmother around that time of year. No matter what pain I was going through. She could make me feel like I was loved. My husband and children do that for me now unconditionally. I must admit though at times I yearn for the love of old.

THE DREAM

The first memory I have of my father is standing by an open trunk. He was not there but his art work was. He was supposed to come see me but instead his drawing arrived. I can not remember what the drawing were of but I remember being mad as hell they were so beautiful. Shoot it appeared at the time they must have been more beautiful than I was because he spent time with them and not with me. I remember standing at that trunk and ripping one of the drawings to shreds and crying. I was crying because I was destroying the most beautiful thing I had ever seen created by a person before and I regretted it as I was doing it but I could not stop. I spent most of my life yearning for my father and hoping that he would show up one day and whisk me away to happiness. I was always waiting for him to arrive or call and I could not understand why I was so unworthy of his attention. When I was in elementary school I used to make up stories about he was. They would be quite intriguing stories too, like he was the only black man in the mafia but they could not tell because he looked caecilian. The reality is as a child I had only few minutes of face time with my father. At times I would forget what he would look like because I did not even have a picture. In my mind he was this caramel god, with beautiful hair and eyes that mimicked mine. I used to narrow in on the eyes because that was the only thing that I had that I could not attribute to my mother. My father was a mystery to me and in the beginning the only thing I had was his name. It was the late eighties and early nineties so we did not have the internet then. So in order to find my father I had to do real work. I was in middle school when I began my search. I started asking around my school and found someone related to him. I snuck off one day after school and went to a house that I thought belonged to him but I was wrong. Eventually I found someone who not only knew my father but was able to provide me with the phone number to my older sister. When they say there is only six degrees of separation in this world I learned first hand that was true. I remember holding the paper with my sister's name and number on it in my hand thinking my life was going to change. I called her as soon as I got home and found out some hard truths. My father was in a jail, not for the first time but again. My sister was living with an older man because she could no longer stay with her grandmother. Her mother was in a mental institution and this family that I thought was looking for me knew where I was the entire time. After speaking to my sister I went to my mother to find out if all of this was true and she just told me I could not have a relationship with my sister until I left her house. I did not listen to her though the first chance I got, I went to my sister's house. The first time I saw her I could not imagine we were related. She was beautiful, I was sure she was my sister though because she had eyes like mine.

We sat on her porch and talked for hours and swore we would keep in contact because we were all we had. So I made sure to call her as often as possible but very soon the picture perfect situation he had living with the older man fell apart and I had no way to reach her. I tried visiting few places I thought I would find her but I had no luck. So just remember walking home with tears in my eyes because the only person with any link to my father has slipped away. Loosing my sister was just as painful, having someone to connect as a sibling who knew what of felt like for their father not to be there was something I yearned for. In addition to the fact that I just wanted to love my sister because she was my sister. My siblings with my mother were kept so far away from me like I was pariah she was the only chance I had at having a real sibling relationship.

It took years for me to find my father after that, I used to hope he would just show up one day but it never happened. My freshman year in college I decided I would look for him again; I knew he had been in jail. So I called the county jail and provided his name. I remember that phone call so clearly I was speaking with a very kind man. Who wanted to know why I would be looking for this man, his criminal record was long and I sounded like a nice girl. I explained that he was my father and I really wanted to find him. I will never forget the officer telling me, I was better off not knowing. I Insisted and he provided me with an address and phone number to a half way house. So I called him and the man I spoke to sounded nothing like who I thought would be my father. He was broken and he told me I was not his daughter, that my mother was a liar and whore. He gave me the name of another man who he claimed was my father. I was hysterical and I called my mother because she was the only one who knew the truth. My mother facilitated a three way call with my father where he apologized and said that he was wrong. He was indeed my father but that he was not a good man. That he was trying to learn to be a man and I was better off without him. When that phone call was over I felt like my life was over. The little bit of hope I did have vanished. So I decided that I would not give up, I called him again. This time he spoke with me, told me about my family. He even invited me to come visit him. My boyfriend at the time took me on the two-hour drive to the farm he was staying at that was run by a priest. What I saw when I arrived was a man who was broken and trying to rehabilitate himself. He was learning like Jesus to be carpenter. Those were his words not mine, but he in reality had noting to offer me. He showed me the few pictures he had of me and my sister. Gave me a tour of the carpenter shop and showed me where he painted. Before I left that day he gave me a few drawing he had made simply with pencil. They were amazing and in fact I still have them to this day. I gave him my number asked him to call me and try to build some type of relationship with me. The call never came and I never went back. I saw my father again shortly before I was about to get married he was walking down the street with his girlfriend. I was with my fiancé and he stopped me, gave me a hug and told me how proud he was of me. I did not invite him to my wedding and my husband was disgusted with him. I secretly wanted to ask him to walk me down the isle because I did not want my stepfather to do it. I never did and the reality is the next time I saw my father I had been married for two years.

At times I find myself bombarded with phone calls in regards to the sister that I don't really know. I am not sure if I should be angry or feel sorry for her. Obviously they feel as if I should be concerned for this woman and her children. Someone even went as far as to send me a prayer in an e-mail in regarding her. So I ask is family only a blood connection? If that is the case, then I should be inclined to be up in arms about this situation. However, up until this point these people have reached out to me more about her issues than they have contacted me in my entire life. I did not hear from these people for any of my birthdays ever, graduations, my wedding or the birth of my children! Now for some reason I am supposed to act for them in regard to a situation that I really don't have any real information about. I am thinking that because I have all this "education" they think that I have the answers they are seeking. Knowing nothing about me which was clear in they way they were behaving. If they knew me they would know my struggle and refrain from sending birth announcements via text messages. I did not even know that my sister was pregnant until I received the message from my father. Who I had not heard from my father in three years up until that point. It did not matter that I was trying to get pregnant at the time. I was always trying to be a good person and provide to others the same considerations that I would like. However, I grew up without a father and his side of my family. Regardless of the fact that they lived around the corner from me. They never spoke to me or tried to find me, now as a successful adult I am supposed to want to help.

So I struggle with this family issue because I have so many people that are considered family that have never been a real part of my life. I have friends that are not related to me by blood that have been in my life, living with me for as long as I can remember. I have blood family members that have hurt me or allowed me to be hurt in order to maintain their happiness. So family and this idea that blood is thicker than water is sickening to me. We may share the same blood but we are not family. I can not be expected to act on your behalf just because we share the same blood. When none of the attributes of family have ever been extended to me. I actually used to work with one of my cousins everyday and did not know we were related. Those are the type of situations that make me so angry, I could have had and ally or family. That never happened for me and I was not in control of the situation, my father did one thing for me in my life that I remember and it helped me to leave my home state for the second time. I was graduating from grad school and desperate for money. I was just learning a very hard lesson about transitioning from graduate school to the teaching world. I called him to tell him I was leaving and he told me to come by before I left. I brought my son over to meet him and he gave me two hundred dollars to help with my travel expenses. He promised to mail me some paintings but he never did. After that day I never heard from my father again while he was alive. Three years later I received a call from a maternal cousin that my father had died and his family was looking for me. That moment was three years ago today and it is as if I can still feel the anguish that crept slowly through my body. I thought we had more time, that one day he would get it together and my children would call him granddaddy and I would have a chance to call him daddy. We did not have later, I was his next of kin and had to go home and bury my father. The man who from what I can recall only ever gave me 2 hugs and two hundred dollars in my lifetime. I actually remember one of my old school mates contacting me on Facebook when I posted that my father died. He had no idea that I was not talking about my stepfather. I had to explain to him who my father really was. My husband and we took the fourteen-hour drive back home to settle my father's affairs. In his death I have spent more time with my father than I did while he was still on this earth. I was able to go through all his paperwork and see the life lived without me. With the help of his sisters, brother and girlfriend I planned my father funeral. It took me a week but I found his life insurance policy and I was able to afford a nice home going for him. I stood and I was the last person to speak at my father's funeral and it was there that I forgave him and thanked him for letting me be. There were so many people there for my father and most of them did not know I existed. I stood in front of them and the air seemed to disappear from the room. I was having a panic attack but I had to say what was on my heart. So I locked eyes with my husband and spoke my truth. It was not horrible but it was sad and true. While he was on this earth we did not have the time to connect. I always thought there would be more time but that we had no control of. Most of them knew a different man than I did, one who had changed his life. He was a successful carpenter and a hard working man. I never got to meet the man they knew and it is and was unfair. He grew up and became a man which in my mind means he could have become a father to me. It never happened though and in my heart I am still that rejected little girl waiting for my father to show up and call me his princess. It is too late now and I know those word will never fall from his lips and as I mourn my father, I mourn the hopes and dreams I had of my father. My father's ashes still remain with me until this day. I can't bring myself to part with them or look at them. I keep telling myself I have more time. That one day I will figure out what to do with his ashes and I will feel liberated. I don't know what the truth is, I just know that I spent thirty-three years waiting to spend time with my father. So it may take me thirty-three years to spread his ashes. He is with me now and no one can change that but me. It is an odd type of power to have because those ashes can't talk back to me. I did finally get to call him daddy though. I wrote it on his face book wall after the funeral. Now I have moments that I just hope he loved me and that I hope he really was my father. The result of my father's death has been a connection with one of his sister and a few cousins. It is a good thing but difficult at the same time because I am not used to having these people in my life. I often can't understand why now is the time to connect instead of when I was child. I have made my peace with them though and the relation ship we have is evolving as I evolve. I have learned I can't blame anyone for my fathers lack of ability to be a real father. We all have the things that exist in our lives that at the moment seem more important than anything or anyone. Knowing that I have nieces and nephews who have never known me and there is a possibility they never will puts it all in perspective. Is it possible for me to be upset at someone for not doing for me what I have not done for my own nieces and nephews? I guess that is the problem with being a fatherless child. It has an impact far beyond you, it impacts generations of children that don't even know the problem.

THE SILENCE

I know that I could have done this differently but I had to do this my way. I have been speaking for years about how damaging silence is and what damage it has done to my life. So when it was time to share the things that I felt held me hostage, I wanted to make sure I did it my way. The Silence No More project is a product of my lived experience. Each chapter of this book has a video that will accompany it and you can see me talking on how the silence associated with these issues have been damaging to my life. I know I have said it before but I was told my whole life I talked too much. So I spent so much time trying to be quiet and hold back so I could be seen as good and likable. It is very difficult to spend your time trying to make sure you don't do what comes natural to you. To remain quiet and not share who you are with the world even though you really want to share. The idea that what you have to say is not valuable or worth hearing. I know many of us grew up hearing that kids are meant to be seen and not heard. Many adults took that saying way too far. Noelle-Neumann said that, social sanctions play a key role, and silence can occur when opinions concerning topics that are perceived to be controversial and divisive are shared with at least one other person (Rebirth, 2007, cited in Heney, 2011). Society threatens individuals with isolation, and so cohesion in the social collective must be constantly ensured by a sufficient level of agreement on values and goals Noelle-Neumann, 1991:258). Individuals fear becoming 'social isolates' (Sanders et al., 1985: xvi). Based on their perception of the climate of opinion, people will be willing or reluctant to speak out have the willingness to speak out on their issues, the minority groups remain silent due to a fear of isolation. (Oh, 2011:2). "Introduced in 1974, The spiral of silence is a mass communication theory introduced by Elizabeth Noelle-Neumann (1974) to describe the process of public opinion formation. Noelle-Neumann defines the "spiral of silence" as the process an individual experience when "he may find that the views he holds are losing ground; the more this appears to be so, the more uncertain he will become of himself, and the less he will be inclined to express his opinion" (p. 44). I said that all to provide credibility what many of us know already. Silence causes isolation in individuals, specifically in those a position where they don't have a voice about issues that impact them personally. As a child if you feel like you can tell your parents about someone hurting you, you are far less likely to become a victim. Most children have no idea that there is a possibility they wont be protected. I was shocked when I told my mother and nothing happened because she was the primary person that I looked to for protection. The fact that I told her and she did nothing was the first step in silencing me. My father was not present so I would have had to build up the courage to turn to a stranger. Who would that stranger be? That is a question that as a child

I sat and thought about more nights than I can count. Who was I going to go to protect me if the one person who I though would guarantee my safety decided they were not going to help me. No one can get close and those that y our do let in don't stay long. They see you as a person who is lost and never understand why you don't just leave. My mother would always find a reason why others were not good for me to hang around. Afraid that others would know what she allowed to happen. I lost the person who played the role of protector in my life. The spiral of silence theory is one that explores hypotheses to determine why some groups remain silent while others are more vocal in forums of public discourse. The theory contends that the silence displayed by certain groups is due to the unpopularity of their opinions in the public sphere. While the majority groups are supported by and consequently have the willingness to speak out on their issues" (Neil, 2009). It must be said that cultural factor affect how silence is used. Ones cultural values can determine if you will or will not speak out about an issue. I have people in my family that even until this day say that my abuse is a private matter. I was advised by an aunt not to even share it with my husband because it should stay in the family. The silence that existed in my life was created by the culture I lived in. The values that were instilled in me as child. It was my job to protect my family from the outside world by keeping this secret and if I did not my life was guaranteed to change. This change that I would have had to experience seemed like it would be the end of my life. I was a kid and my world was so small that I did not even have another adult that I trusted enough to share what was happening to me. Trust is one of those qualities that I still have a difficult time understanding today. As I got older and left home I shared with several family members my abuse. Some of them doubted my story in my face and others said that they had to be loyal to my mother so what I shared was irrelevant. These people still until this day talk with, eat and share memories with a child molester, in fact my mother is still married to and lives with him. I have even had family members say they were upset that it happened to me but they still have a relationship with and deal with my abuser. As far as friends are concerned I had a friend who told her mother about my situation. Her mother confronted my mother but never called the police. After that situation my mother reconfirmed that she did not want me sharing our business. I remember actually sitting in the room while my mother and stepfather went crazy because my little sister told them someone at her daycare center touch her in the bathroom. They called the police and went up to the the childcare center. I was amazed that I was not just as important as she was to my mother. It was a lesson in how much value I had, I was not as important as my sister was. Now I can't say for a fact that was the intent but as a child that is what I took from the situation. The one message that was repeatedly sent to me was that I did not have the right to share with the world that I was being victimized because I was not important enough to care about. So silence existed for me inside of every area of my life. My self worth was tied to that silence and the longer I remained silent the less I thought I was worth. The other part of this was the idea that I was a liar and a liar is never worth listening to anyway. I am the first to admit that as a child I had an active imagination. I made up stories about thing that would never be true but to think that I made up the trauma I was experiencing is insane. So I wore the scarlet letter of liar for a long time. It made me feel like no one would believe anything I said anyway. I tried to make sure that I backed up everything I said with facts and evidence. To many that made me appear as if I was always trying to be smarter than everyone else. The reality of my life is I did have to lie. I lied about seeing my father, family vacation, activities with my family and things that I thought normal people did. I lied because I was doing what I was told, keeping our business out of the street. You see in order to have to remain quiet about what was happening to me, I had to make up events that occurred instead. Let me clarify I did not have to make them up but I was smart enough to know those lies were necessary for my family to appear normal. As an adult I look at my children and I know they tell tall tales but liars they are not. They spin the tales that children spin and it is easy to know the difference. The label of liar is one that is often given to victims of abuse, it is done to reduce their credibility and make other less likely to listen to them. I also want to point out that this silence I was living in was also perpetuated by that fact that my stepfather was not the only abuser in my family. I had to deal with other men in my family who were abusive sexually and mentally abusive to me. As I look back now I see that there was so much silence and pain being modelled for me that I had no other way to go. I want everyone to know that this is not something that I am making up in my head. As a communications professor I have been studying this for ten years. Just waiting for the opportunity to express myself and make these two issues become important. We can have had all the walks, dances, fundraiser and support groups to help victims. If no feel like they can really speak out, then we are not helping them. The reality is that the abuser should be the person afraid to speak. This fear I speak of is not fear you might have as a fleeting experience, this is a heavy and dominating fear. It prevents you from moving forward in your life because you feel you must remain silent about certain situations that existed it in your life. Especially when it explains why you are now who you are. When I think of my silence I see how it was a catalyst for me to stand in the back and not participate in events or projects because I was still hiding. It becomes a pattern of life that you exist in. The irrational fear of weather the information you provide could shatter the world around you and make you look incompetent. It is so much easier to pretend to be invisible. To be alone so that no can hear you speak, simple acts that many take for granted like inviting someone into their home for coffee. The silence touched that act because it is not enough to remain silent you can not show visual signs that there is a problem. So you stop inviting people in you home so that the cannot see your dysfunctions. When I was in high school and feeling a bit rebellious I joined this support group in high school. I shared in that group my dilemma the issues I was dealing with. The responses I got from my peers made me feel like silence was the best option. They made it seem like I was deciding to remain in a bad situation that I had options. They had no real idea of what the silence did to me. No one can get close and those that you do let in don't stay long. They see you as a person who is lost and never understand why you don't just leave. My mother would always find a reason why others were not good for me to hang around. Afraid that others would know what she allowed to happen. The rejection from my peers further confirmed that I should have kept my mouth shut. As an adult that translate to a fear of inviting people in your home, not because you have a secret anymore. You manufacture reason, like my house is good enough. My furniture is old or my kids might misbehave. In order for someone to come into your world everything has to be perfect so no sees that there could possibly be any flaws. You are still protecting a secret that does not exist anymore. It is exhausting because in reality you being silent with your family as well.

They have no idea why you never want to go places or invite people over. In fact, I used to clean for hours if I had an inclination that someone might come to my house. It would frustrate my husband because he had no idea what was going on with me. I was still keeping my secret and I was doing a good job of being silent. The thing is the silence slowly starts to eat away at you, silent panic attack seems to others that you are ignoring them. When you are just trying to cope, but it is a secret so no one knows. So you suffer in silence and accept that you are just a bad person because you are hurting the people you love. I knew my silence had to stop in order for me to exist any longer in this world. I credit my children with the fact that I am still here today. I never wanted them to suffer because of me so I refrained from killing myself. When I found my voice and I mean really found my voice my life changed. After living with silence for so long, your voice can be really scary. At times I would wonder if I was talking or was I pretending to be who I wanted to be. Eventually after therapy and time I started to see myself. To see that my voice had the ability to change. Once you see your voice as a change agent, you begin to get some of your power back. When I stand in front of the classroom I use my voice to provide a perspective to the young people who will run this world one day. I speak of love all the time, unconditional love and I hope that they remember me for it. That they carry with them my voice for a little while and it makes a difference in their lives. I am not conceited enough to think that I will touch every person I meet and make a difference. It does not matter if I touch one than the gift I was given that I kept hidden for so long is being used for good. I know now the best thing about me is my voice. I have been given a gift from God to express myself. This is for me this book; this project is for me. It is my opportunity to shout to the world that I have a voice and I will use it. I will say that my stepfather molested me. I will say that I am a fatherless child. I will say that I have an eating disorder. I will say that I suffered from PTSD. Those things have made me who I am today and you can't really know who I am or what I stand for without knowing those thing. After reading this I hope that you will not pity me, I have been lucky. I survived everything that I have been through. I have survived and been successful in my life despite the circumstances. If you can take anything from this take the fact that I am no longer silent as proof. It is evidence that your voice matters and that you need to allows others to have a voice. We live in a world where we see and hear horrible things happening on television and the news everyday. We talk about those things but hide the terrible and horrific things that are happening in our homes. We silence children and tell them to keep secrets that become burdens that too large for them to carry. I have witnessed people express outrage on Facebook, twitter and message boards about the horrific state of the world and still be afraid to say they were victims of sexual abuse or domestic violence. Many of us may never have the chance to change to world, stop wars or end hunger. What we do have the ability to do is save our children and stop the cycle of habitual silence in our community. That seems to me to be at the root of the increased amount of violence and mental illness we are experiencing in this world today. People are suffering in silence and it manifest its self in their actions and then something terrible happens and we all wonder why? When saying you have been raped, abused or are mentally ill is met with so much stigma. People will troll the internet looking for reasons why victims are liars and attack them over and over again. The twenty-four-hour news cycle perpetuates this media frenzy where everyone feels they have right to comment on someone lses pain. Look at Face book for instance in your timeline you see memes, real people in pictures being used for entertainment. Without their consent people share them and repeat put them out into the world as a joke. Every time I see one of those pictures my heart aches because I don't know the story behind the person in the picture. Now they are just a joke and when they speak up the world silences them by making more memes and posting cruel comments about the picture. I know it might seem like I am going on a tangent but I am not. I just gave real life example of how we silence people we don't even know. Why speak up if within twenty-four hours your life will be a meme or being examined on television by people who have no idea what you have been through. It is all a part of the spiral of silence that we ignore blatantly everyday. As an adult I spend a tremendous amount of time reflecting on my childhood. Reflecting more because I don't want to forget. Reflecting because I want my children to have a better one than I did. As Mother's Day approaches, I look at my children and hope. I hope than when they are my age, they will look back in love at our relationship. Mothers day for me is a battle. Should I call her and pretend that, the years of abuse she ignored don't matter anymore. Should I call her and say thank you for having me. For having me even though I am a constant reminder of your rapist. My abuser was never punished for his crime and I left but he was able to resume life. To stay with his family and pretend that he was father of the year. I live with the pain, guilt and regret and silence. I love my siblings and I don't want them to loose their father and become the fatherless child I am. He was able to abused me because I was not his child, my father was not there to protect and silence aided him in his abuse.

I grew up without a father and with a mother that I felt hated me. As an adult I look back and realize that I was a constant reminder of her rape. What I can't understand is, if she knew that pain. I mean if she knew that pain, why would she let me suffer, the same. Then allow me to live in a daily hell, of seeing my abuser. It is almost like, if she was going to suffer than I should suffer.

I know a lot of people; I am friends with lots of people Facebook. The problem is that I don't feel Like I have any real friends. Sometimes when the chips are down and I need a secure, strong shoulder there is no one to call except my husband. I can remember when I really had friends, I think I was in middle school. Back then I had a strong group of young ladies to hang out with and we really cared about each other. In high school, I began to feel how different I was. I struggled aimlessly to fit into several different groups. Most of which I never really belonged.

I carried a secret that I kept hidden and failed to share with many people. When I did share, I faced adolescent critics that thought there was an easy answer to my monumental problem. It made me hide from other people, I never really wanted them to see me for who I really was. I think that feeling has traveled into my adult years, I have failed to really find friends and I tend to keep people at a distance. I don't want to be that way, so I am trying to open up a bit more each day. The funny things are that people who really don't know me describe me as a social butterfly. I laugh at that description because talking to people in groups is very superficial and it is a skill that I have. To communicate with others is the gift I was born with. I am passionate to a fault about motivating others in life. It does not mean that I have close friendships or relationships. You have to be open for that to occur and every time I have been open, pain followed.

Like a scared little girl sometimes I am afraid to invite people to my home. Still afraid of the secrets they might see or that they might be tarnished by the same plaque I was. Even though now my home is safe, I have made sure of that. It is a delightful refuge full of laughter and the noise of happy rowdy children. Old habits die-hard I guess. As a grown woman I yearn for a grown woman friends. Ones to share my life with, in person not in a Facebook group or on a long distance phone call. To welcome in to my home and enjoy a glass of wine or tea and complain, laugh, gossip and be real. I have had these relationships start before but cross-country moves have prevented them from flourishing. With the lack of family in my life, these relationships are very important to keeping you sane. As women and mothers we give so much of our selves selflessly to our family. You never think about it except in those moments when you are flaming mad and pissed at everyone for taking you for granted. I realize now that I must open my door and let other women in, to see me. That my home may not be perfect every time and neither will my children but I need people too. I can't just spend my time being inspirational to others and never feeling inspiration myself. In away it makes me feel fraudulent that I may not even be taking my own advice. Change is good and I am changing my life.

I still have days where I wake up thinking of a way out of the things I planned for the day. It seems much more appealing to hide under the covers for most of the day with only my thoughts and possibly a book or an iPad. Some mornings I can't bear to face the world. Anxiety can be so strong. It steels your joy and controls your body. I feel it more now in my stomach but I fight it most of the time. I find myself looking for relief from the tightness in my chest and stomach that sometimes it makes it difficult to eat. Food just sits in my stomach like a weight that does not sink. It floats up to my chest and sits in my throat. Days like that I wish I could go back in time to when I was a kid and walk into a police station. To tell someone the hell I was living in and end my silence. For years I felt like I did not tell for my siblings so that they could have the life I never had. Now I see that really did not matter I am an outsider, outside the family and it may remain that way. The thing is I am in recovery and changing my life, it is difficult. I do know that I live a good life with or without them. There are moments, terrifying moments when I face the things I fear. Like looking incompetent in front of important people, or brain farts that just happen. Those moments when for a brief second I think I have to be perfect in this life. Then I remember that I know that no one is perfect but those moments are scary, thanks to recovery my imposter syndrome has left with the silence. I guess it is the fear that someone might find out that I am as flawed as I feel. To have the world think that I am not perfect. The reality is that I am not perfect and I am now okay with that. The thing about silence is when you exist in it the way I did, feeling anything about yourself is horrifying. Along with idea of socializing with those excruciatingly happy people, that seem that way because you are so sad. I am sensible and motivational to my friends, family, students and even strangers. That is just what I want to bring to the world, to be the positive moment in each day. Hoping if just for moment that if someone one feels the way I do, I will bring light where darkness lives. It so hard to understand how the traumas of childhood can cause so much pain in adulthood. I woke up this morning with a tiny ache in my heart and by mid afternoon it had engulfed me to tears. The feeling of isolation as a result of "telling" follows me. In the future I won't see my mother, brother, sister or niece. They will be with my abuser and it is unfair but I can't live in that pain anymore.

I know I have upset some of my family by telling my truth and refusing to remain quiet about the abuse. The abuse I suffered at the hands of my step-father for longer than I can remember. The thing is I won't waiver, it is painful but what I went through as a child was horrendous. It stole my spirit and darkened my heart, as result I learned to hide. Hide from everyone, so they would not be able to see the real me. This is a difficult journey that I am on, walking out of the shadows of years of silence. Sometimes I just I let the tears replenish my strength for the day and I am grateful for them. I am changing and the change is beautiful, I am in recovery, I love myself, my voice is loud and I have a family. Nothing else matters…

ABOUT THE AUTHOR

Kenisha Burke is a wife, mother, sister and friend. Her passion is showing others that love is the answer to finding their happiness. She is also a college professor and motivational speaker who has spent ten years on this project to make sure everyone has a chance to have their voices heard.

http://iwillbesilentnomore.org

www.ingramcontent.com/pod-product-compliance
Ingram Content Group UK Ltd.
Pitfield, Milton Keynes, MK11 3LW, UK
UKHW041937190726
13854UKWH00004B/1641